Mount Your Own Fish Trophies

W. E. Moore

ILLUSTRATIONS BY THE AUTHOR

DOUBLEDAY & COMPANY, INC.
Garden City, New York

Library of Congress Cataloging in Publication Data

Moore, William, 1914–
   Mount your own fish trophies.

    1. Fishes—Collection and preservation. 2. Taxidermy. I. Title.
QL618.6M66   579'.4
ISBN 0-385-03532-2
Library of Congress Catalog Card Number 74–4831

CONTENTS

PART I

Basics

As a taxidermist over the past thirty-five years, I have had scores of requests from fishermen—boys, men, *and* women—to teach them how to mount their own fish. Generally these good people had already caught the specimen that they desired to keep, but they were not in a position to spend the money to have a professional taxidermist do the job for them. Of course, some of them simply preferred that pride of accomplishment that they might get from seeing their own efforts displayed on the wall of their study or den.

Very few of these folks had any notion of how much work, time, and practice might be necessary in order to have results of which they could truly be proud. Many of them had a vague idea that this art is something of an "embalming" process . . . that you merely "soak" the fish in some solution—or "inject" him and then screw him onto a board and let him dry! One such person called me in May of last year asking for a "cram" course for his daughter and himself in preparation for a June Alaskan trip in which they intended to mount 'em as they caught 'em. Needless to say, such a "course" would be absolutely impossible, and I would have been accepting his money under false pretenses had I undertaken to prepare him for such a thing.

Others have called me frequently to learn just how they should care for their anticipated trophies until they could reach home and find a good taxidermist. At any rate—and for whatever reason—I decided to work out a brief course that would be desirable for these folks . . . as nearly as possible, a foolproof—*simple*—method of mounting small and medium-sized fish with a minimum of tools, equipment, or other paraphernalia so that the beginner would have a chance of success on his very first fish!

Experimentally, I have used this method with a number of students, ranging in ages from twelve through eighty-three, and *every last one* of them finished with a fish that he or she had caught and mounted, and, most of all, that he or she could be proud to display—as good a job as many done by so-called professionals!

Now a word of advice. Each of these students had one thing in common: a desire to really do their work *and* an ability to follow instructions. If you can do that, if you have a little native mechanical ability (like doing things with your hands), you can turn the pages of this little book and expect to find some degree of satisfaction in mounting your own fish! If you have some artistic ability as well—or are meticulous in making notes and observations—you may well be on your way to doing outstanding work on your own fish and those of your friends as well.

Whatever your reason for undertaking this bit of taxidermy work, you will find that *practice* is the big item in the amount of success that you will have. Second, bear in mind that fish are fairly fragile creatures that cannot be thrown about like a carpet without losing their scales or splitting their fins or tails; neither can these delicate appendages be folded or rolled without ruining them as well as the finished product. Treat 'em easy! With this in mind, let's proceed to the work at hand.

I can recall that the first fish I ever "mounted," when I was a young boy, was a small-mouthed bass. I'd never had any instructions whatever, but I had sense enough to know that you had to get the meat and stuff out of him somehow; you had to preserve the skin and then "stuff" him with something or other that wouldn't rot. With that in mind, I opened his mouth and skinned him, using a small pair of scissors thrust down into his gullet— that and his gill covers. I simply reached in, chopped up everything, and dragged it out. With that accomplished, I layered his insides heavily with salt, figuring that as all farm folks know, salt will preserve *anything* if you use enough of it. All of this seemed reasonable enough, so I next dug some good red clay out of that Lawrence County hillside and proceeded to "stuff" old Mr. Small-mouth through the same opening that I had removed him from—his mouth! Naturally, I had no seams to sew up, and before the afternoon was over, I had him posed and drying in true "fighting" form on the top of an old cedar fence post.

Needless to say, there was much to be desired in my first results, but basically what I did there forty-odd years ago was what is necessary for you to do to mount your fish: (1) catch him; (2) skin him; (3) preserve the skin; (4) make an artificial body; (5) stretch the skin over this body and fasten it in place; (6) pose the fish and let it dry; (7) retouch the colors that have faded, and finally (8) mount it on a suitable panel.

WHICH FISH TO USE

For practical purposes, this study deals only with fish such as perch, bluegills, crappies, bass, walleyes, etc. Avoid choosing such specimens as catfish, trout, spoonbills, sturgeon, carp, and suckers; these latter fish will get so involved with their special problems that your first effort will likely be your last one. Nothing is better to work on than a real nice crappie or, say, about a four-

teen-inch or sixteen-inch large-mouth. While pike have a good tough hide on them, the beginner will find it difficult to wrestle them around without losing a good many scales and all of his patience. Whatever the species, *stick to one of medium size.*

TOOLS AND EQUIPMENT

Very few tools are needed to begin with. Most of them can be found around the average household. If you have access to a little corner of the garage or basement where you have a sink and running water, you will save many steps. (A kitchen will also do nicely if you can convince the proprietor of same that what you are about to undertake is no messier than preparing a fish for the frying pan.) The ordinary tools of any home workshop will have a way of suggesting themselves as various stages of your work progress.

For *skinning,* you will need:

1. A pair of stout-handled, short-bladed scissors. For many years I have used the same old scissors—a pair of barber shears that I shortened the blades on to about 1½ inches. I do 90 per cent of my skinning with these. (See sketch, Plate 1.)

2. A pair of six-inch or eight-inch diagonal cutters to clip out bones, trim the spines on fin butts, etc.

3. A dull kitchen knife to scrape fat and tissue from the skin.

4. A pair of pliers with a wire cutter on the jaws.

5. A wire coat hanger—to clip into convenient hooks to clean out cheek muscles, etc.

6. *Either* a needle assortment and stout thread *or* a staple gun—depending on whether you wish to sew up your specimen or staple his skin in place on the back side. (I prefer the latter.)

7. A sharp knife for carving the artificial body.

8. A wood rasp and some sandpaper.

9. A small hand-drill.

10. A plastic pan or tray that will accom-

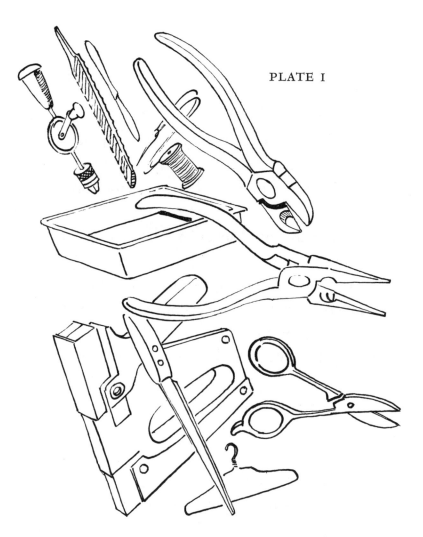

PLATE I

modate your fish without bending him in any way (a kitty-litter pan will do very well); do not use a metal pan unless you protect it with a sheet of plastic. Also provide yourself with a piece of plastic or oilcloth to cover the tray to prevent evaporation in case you keep the specimen for some time after skinning it.

With these tools at hand, you are ready to start on your fish.

SKIN PRESERVATIVE

Although you will not need a preservative until you have actually skinned your fish, it is well

PLATE 2

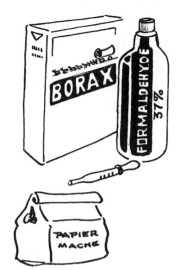

to have it on hand and available as soon as you need it.

Throughout my career, I've used many different formulations, some that were terribly poisonous and dangerous to use—foolish formulas containing such awful things as arsenic that should never be kept about. *Never* attempt to use such stuff! Some supply houses recommend their own products of one kind or another, saying that these tend to preserve the natural colors, etc. I have found *nothing* that will do this! My experience has been that *all* fish colors will fade and have to be retouched later. I have found that the following recipe does do a good job; it is simple to remember; the ingredients are readily available;

and it is safe to use, even though it too contains a poisonous ingredient, *formaldehyde.**

The ingredients are:

1. Powdered borax—the 20-Mule Team variety. Not Boraxo, but the common old wash-product, *borax.*

2. Formaldehyde—the 37 per cent variety sold in drugstores.

3. Water—I prefer soft water such as rain-water, but plain old tap water will do.

---

* *Formaldehyde,* when mixed with water, is generally referred to as "Formalin." In some areas, it may be found on the shelf by both names. Ordinarily the terms are used interchangeably.

Mix as follows:

For each quart of water, stir into it one large handful of dry borax. Stir until it is largely dissolved; then add one medicine dropper of formaldehyde. Stir it about with a wooden paddle and it is ready to receive your fish skin. Avoid breathing the fumes of the formaldehyde. Also avoid unnecessary contact with your skin. Common-sense usage of *all* powders and caustics is in order.

This is the only recipe that you will need in this bit of work.

THE ACTUAL MOUNTING

1. You will notice shortly after catching your fish that the colors on it will change noticeably. If you are seriously interested in restoring these *same* fresh colors, you should make some notes that will help you, and make them as descriptive as possible while still in the field. If it is not possible for you to begin work on the fish at once, make your notes as complete as you can before putting him away. (See Plate 3.)

Incidentally, if you *must* put off working on him for some time, wrap him carefully in a plastic bag and put him in the deep freeze—he can be kept for several weeks in this way, but *do not* gut him or remove the gills. Put a couple of layers of wet paper towels over his tail and fins to keep them from freeze-drying; then, when you are ready to proceed, just thaw him out and work as though he were a freshly caught fish.

Wash the fish in cool, clean water; put it un-

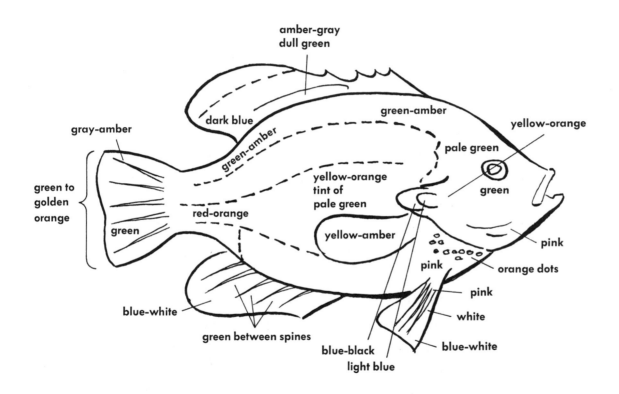

amber-gray
dull green

gray-amber

dark blue

green-amber

green-amber

green to
golden
orange

red-orange

green

yellow-orange
tint of
pale green

pale green

yellow-orange

green

yellow-amber

pink

orange dots

pink

blue-white

pink

white

green between spines

blue-black

light blue

blue-white

PLATE 3

A nice winter bluegill

der the tap and flush all slime and mucus from the surface, mouth, and gill openings. Hold him by the jaw so that the water will drain toward the tail—use a bit of paper towel to loosen any clinging foreign matter. Remember: any scales that are loose or that you dislodge will most certainly be obviously missing on your finished specimen, so treat 'em easy!

2. Examine your fish carefully: In mounting this fish, one side of it will be against the wall or a panel; naturally, any blemishes or scars should be turned to that side so that they will not show. The best side will be facing up, so place your fish on a large piece of paper (a grocery sack will do nicely) and pose him on this paper in as nearly the position you wish to have him mounted as possible. If the mouth is to be open, prop it in position with a wad of paper. Then, holding a pencil straight up and down—following the outline of the fish—make an outline drawing of him on the paper. Use care in doing this—check and recheck, for this outline will become a guide from which you will later make an artificial body. (See Plate 4.)

3. In case you did *not* make notes on the coloration of your fish when you brought him out of the water, now is the time to do this. Make a second outline drawing of him; spread the fins and include them. On this drawing, describe as accurately as possible all colors that you will later retouch. (See Plate 3.)

4. Now you are ready to turn the fish over and

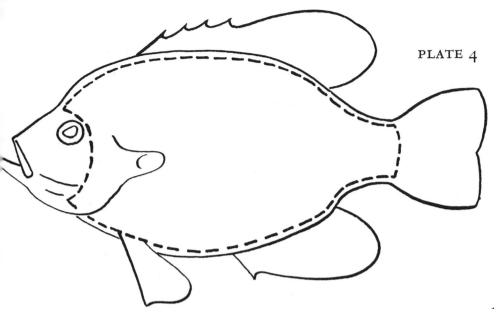

PLATE 4

As indicated by the dotted line—allowing for the skin's thickness—you will later make your artificial body. Take time to make it as accurately as possible.

commence the skinning operation. Before doing *so and at all times during the skinning process,* moisten the entire fish, especially the fins and tail —and *keep them moist.* I find it to great advantage to do my actual skinning on a large platter or other very smooth surface that can be kept wet. This allows the fish to be moved without fear of rubbing any scales loose. (The bottom of your plastic tray will do well for this.)

5. The dotted lines in Plate 5 indicate the only incisions that are necessary in skinning your fish. Using your scissors, insert the point into the gill opening on the *back* side of the fish as shown in

PLATE 5

The dotted line A–B indicates the first of the two cuts that you intentionally make in skinning your fish. C–D is the second cut, which gives you access to the "other side."

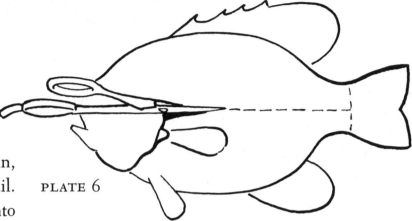

Plate 6. Clipping through the scales and skin, make a single incision from the gills to the tail. Just cut through the skin, but not too deeply into the flesh. Make a second "T" cut at the base of the tail as in the drawing of Plate 6.

PLATE 6

Remember: keep him wet . . . treat him easy. It's hard to replace those scales that pop out if you bend 'em backward!

Holding your scissors parallel to the suface on which you are working, you may easily separate the skin from the flesh, working toward the back fins of the fish along the entire length of its body (See Plate 7.)

Reversing the tray on which you are working, you may also use the scissors to separate the skin from the flesh as you work toward the fins on the

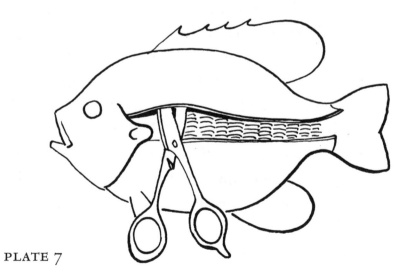

PLATE 7

belly. (See Plate 8.) Keep your fish as nearly flat as you possibly can as you work on him. By turning the tray instead of the fish, you will save a lot of scales that would otherwise be dragged loose.

Upon reaching the dorsal and ventral fins, cut through them with the scissors, leaving considerable flesh on the butts. When the tail has been exposed, carefully clip through the base from the back side until the skin on the front side is exposed; this will leave the tail dangling rather loosely, and this will be the moment when you *must be careful not to dislodge the small scales in this area!* (See Plate 9.)

Your first inclination will be to use this dangling bit of skin as a handle to raise the fish so that you can see what is going on underneath. *Don't*

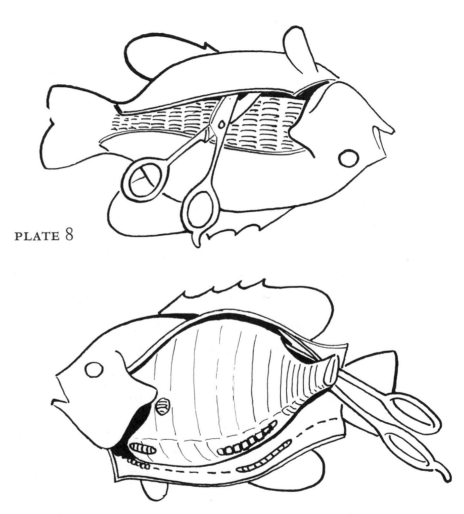

PLATE 8

PLATE 9

do it! Keep that fish lying as nearly flat as you can. Hold the flesh of the body *up* as you reach *under,* and clip the connective tissues with your scissors—only raise the flesh enough to allow you to reach under as you clip. (If you bend the skin backwards, you most assuredly will dislodge the scales.)

At this point, don't worry about leaving a little flesh on the skin; it can be scraped off later, but a hole cannot!

Continue snipping along the underside, belly, and back until you reach the gill collar. Be careful not to cut through the skin behind the fins just in back of the gills—cut deeply into their roots and leave them firmly seated on the skin.

At this point, you may use your diagonal cutters to sever the spine directly behind the head and remove the main portion of the body from the skin. This will leave the head and skin attached, as in the drawing in Plate 10.

You may now lay the body aside while you return to the skin and head.

Keep those fins moist!

6. Rinse your fish skin now as well as your tray, and turn to the job of scraping all the fat and tissue from the interior of the skin. Use a dull knife for this purpose, and always scrape from the tail *toward* the head to keep from popping the scales from their sockets. Remember: Treat him easy!

Trim up the fin and tail butts, leaving only enough bony tissue to give support to these ap-

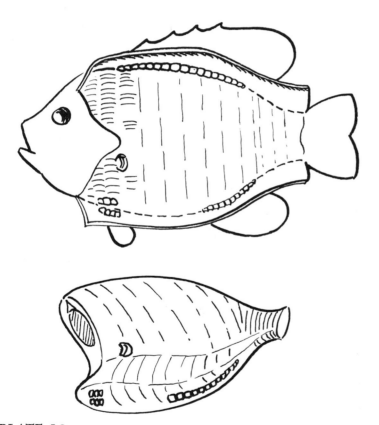

PLATE 10

pendages when they are posed in place on their artificial body.

7. Now turn your attention to the head and gills. This does *not* mean that you will forget the body skin. It of course is still attached to the head and must be handled as carefully as before.

On many fish, you may rely very largely on your scissors to clip out all the flesh and cartilage in the back part of the head; of course, this is now readily exposed and is just a matter of carefully clipping and snipping until all is removed down to the skull. Here you may find it necessary to use your diagonal cutters or pliers to crush and remove the brain case.

At this point, you may well wonder just how much bony tissue to remove. As you will observe, most of those fish that I suggested at the outset of this lesson have very bony heads with the skin tightly anchored to it. Leave only enough of the bony structure to allow the *skin to retain its shape*. Don't attempt to remove the entire skull—but don't leave a lot of fatty, bony tissue to later soak through your fish and discolor it.

A good rule of thumb here: "When in doubt, take it out!"

You will notice that the cheeks of your specimen will have a soft layer of muscle lying between the outer skin and the inner cheek. This will shrink and give your fish a gaunt appearance if left in—unless of course, it is a small fish. This cheek muscle can easily be removed from behind by clipping an incision in the rear of the cheek on the *inside*. Then, using a small hook fashioned from a wire coat-hanger, you may pull or scrape this muscle out from the back side. Later, after you have preserved the skin, this "pouch" may be filled with papier-mâché. (See Plate 11.)

You also have observed by this time that the back sides of the eyes have been exposed. These may be easily removed now. Press against the eye from behind with a finger and as it bulges from its socket, pluck it out from the outside.

Here too, you will give attention to the gills; it's surprising how many people are so concerned about these structures when in life they are only partially visible as the fish breathes. It *is* possible to leave these in place—simply preserving them in the solution used on the skin. It is also very easy

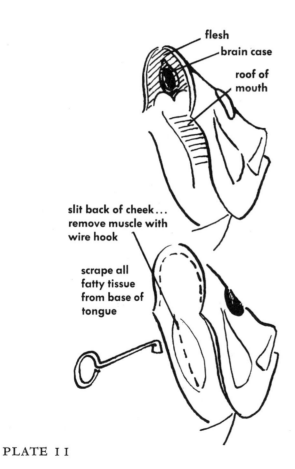

flesh
brain case
roof of mouth

slit back of cheek...
remove muscle with
wire hook

scrape all
fatty tissue
from base of
tongue

PLATE I I

to remove them and later to replace them with papier-mâché that can be effectively modeled to look like the real thing. Or you may simply clip them out and forget them, mounting your fish with the gill covers closed. I suggest the latter course unless you are mounting a large fish in fighting pose with gills extended mightily. As I said before, "When in doubt, take it out."

After finishing with the head, clean out the base of the gill collar and the little bit of meat that extends from below the gills up into the "V" formed by the two sides of the lower jaw. This area of the skin is *extremely* thin and fragile—be careful not to rip it.

You have now completed the skinning of your fish and should rinse it carefully. Check for any spots missed and then immerse it in your tray of preservative solution. Lay it out full length, as nearly as possible in the same position you desire it to be when mounted. If you want the mouth to be opened, do so at this time; spread it and hold it in place with a block of wood.

You will soon note that the preservative has a solidifying action on all tissue. This has a tendency to lock or stabilize the jaws in place. It also will toughen or "rubberize" the skin to some extent. It is also here that you will notice your colors fading perceptively as the skin is "pickled," and the interior will turn white.

Incidentally, the amount of formaldehyde used may make your own skin feel somewhat insensitive, but there is no great harm in this for most normal skin. If you are sensitive to such chemicals, I would recommend that you wear a pair of rubber or plastic gloves during this stage of your work.

Agitate the skin gently in this solution to make sure *all* parts are exposed to the action of the chemicals. Keep it submerged for at least eight or ten hours, moving it about occasionally during this time. After this, the skin may be removed, rinsed, and mounted . . . or, if for any reason you wish to leave it longer, you may simply cover the tray to avoid evaporation and leave the skin in solution until you are ready to continue—even for weeks, if you desire.

So much for the skin. Now we will turn to the making of an artificial body to fit it onto.

THE ARTIFICIAL BODY

Materials

A bit of common sense is in order here. An artificial body can be made from many materials, with the following requirements: They should be light in weight, easily shaped, and durable. My own preference is a type of block "urethane foam." This material seems to be the longest-lasting of the many foam products on the market today, and it is not affected by oils, solvents, or any type of glue that you might use. *Stay away* from the more common styrofoam. It is easily carved and shaped, but it may "melt" away from your fish when you are touching up the colors later on.

A block of balsa wood is a fine material to use if you can find it in sufficient size. It is also desirable in that you will not have to reinforce it with a wooden block, as is the case with the "foams." Neither is it affected by paints, oils, or other finishes. Any other block of soft wood will do as well; such woods as white pine, poplar, or basswood may be desired by some who are adept at handling their harder-carving qualities. Neither will these woods require any kind of reinforcing. Use whichever one is most available in your area.

Assuming that you will use a block of urethane foam (incidentally, many hobby shops sell these blocks, but be sure to use one that is not affected by solvents), study the drawings in Plate 12 carefully.

If you plan to give your fish a curve, be sure

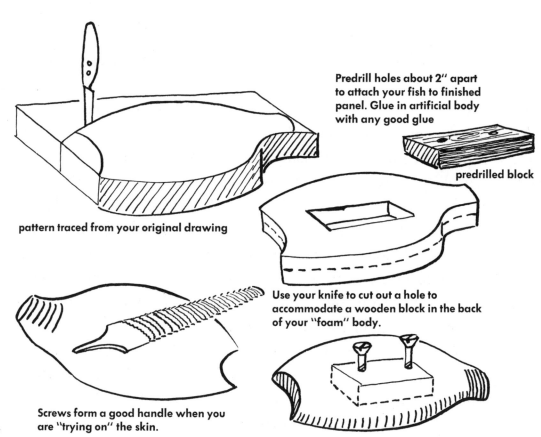

Predrill holes about 2" apart to attach your fish to finished panel. Glue in artificial body with any good glue

predrilled block

pattern traced from your original drawing

Use your knife to cut out a hole to accommodate a wooden block in the back of your "foam" body.

Screws form a good handle when you are "trying on" the skin.

PLATE 12

that you have the tail curved *away* from the wall or panel. Lay a tracing paper over your original drawing of the unskinned fish and, allowing for the approximate thickness of the skin, make a pattern for the body as in Plate 4. Trace this pattern onto your block of foam. Then, with your sharp knife held perpendicular to the block, using a sawing motion, rough out the body. If you do this accurately—which you *must*—both sides of your block will be the same.

Use your knife to "rough away" the excess material, then turn to your rasp to complete the "roughing." Finish your work with a piece of sandpaper.

Now a word of advice: A fish is a *smooth,* streamlined creature, and your success in having such a completed specimen is largely dependent on how well you make this body. If you have kept the old body to this point, unwrap it and make many comparisons with the one you have just made. Take your time, but make it right. When you are satisfied that you have done this, carefully slip the body into the skin, slipping it into the head first and then adjusting the skin around it. If it fits, fine; if it doesn't, remove it and make whatever adjustments are necessary.

Don't wear the skin out trying it on needlessly; remember that it is still a very fragile thing. If you make the body correctly, you will have very little need for any "stuffing" to fake out a poor job, although it is generally necessary to do a little papier-mâché filling around the base of the fins and the butt of the tail.

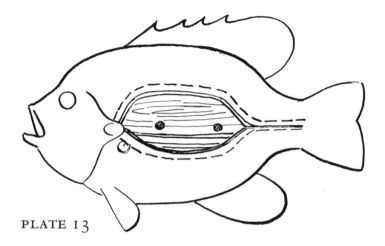

PLATE 13

You have now made all corrections that are necessary, and the skin fits well enough to allow the incisions "A—B" in Plate 5 to close, but *not* to overlap.

Now look at Plate 13 and you will see that an "oval" of skin has been clipped away to expose the reinforcing block of wood and the predrilled screw holes in it. Also note that the fin behind the gill cover has been removed. Since neither of these items will "show," they are not necessary, and if left in place they would interfere with the fish laying close to the panel that it will later be attached to.

You will also notice that the skin in this particular case was stapled in place. You may use this method or you may prefer to sew the skin in place.

Just before putting the skin on its body, wipe all excess moisture from the inside. Mix a small ball of papier-mâché to the consistency of putty. (If no mâché is available, you may substitute potter's clay—have it soft enough to allow some modeling from the outside of the skin.)

Apply a bead of the mâché or clay to *all* fin butts in about the same manner as a generous squeeze from a toothpaste tube onto a brush. Also treat the tail in the same way. While you still have the skin open and the interior of the head is readily accessible, fill the cheeks with mâché so that they will just be smoothly rounded, but not bulged.

Now you are ready to put the skin in place. Many taxidermists use a glue or paste in this step to facilitate the easy moving or adjusting of the skin on the body—as well as to hold it there after drying. In most cases this is not necessary and will only add a note of messiness for the beginner. (If you later decide to try this, use any good paste such as a wheat flour or dextrin base.)

Place the body in the skin and carefully fit it, keeping your beads of mâché where they belong. Use a few straight pins to hold the skin temporarily as you adjust and arrange it. When you are satisfied, staple or sew the incision from the tail toward the head, as in Plate 13. *Carefully model* the mâché now so that your specimen will have no lumps or hollows. Upon completion of this, you will be ready to "mount" your fish on a temporary board or panel. Choose a scrap of wood for this large enough to afford protection for the fins, head, and tail of your work. Run a couple of wood screws through the board into the two pre-drilled holes in your fish. Turn this over now and you will be ready to "card" the fins and tail as in Plate 14.

Wet those fins and tail again now as you study Plate 14 carefully. You will note that two pieces of cardboard have been cut to fit each fin and the tail. Choose smooth cardboard for this so that the drying fins will not stick and be damaged when the cardboards are removed.

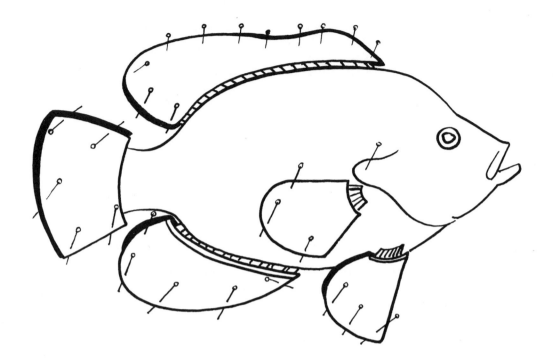

PLATE 14

After you have finished "carding" the fins, you may turn your attention to some of the little details that are necessary before painting your fish.

Secure a pair of glass eyes that will fit your specimen from any taxidermist or supply house such as Van Dyke's of Woonsocket, South Dakota. (See "Troubleshooters' Guide.") Since the eye on the panel side will not show, it is only necessary to "set" one eye in place; save the other for another specimen.

Mix enough papier-mâché to model the inside of the mouth at this time. Fill the eye cavity on the back side so that it will be rounded and smooth. Put enough mâché in the show side to allow you to thrust the little wire attached to the glass eye deep into the eye opening; press the eye down until it takes a natural-looking level. Wipe any excess mâché from around it. You need no glue or other adhesive to do this. The mâché will do the job. You should now set your specimen aside to dry completely. Depending upon its size and the weather conditions, this will require from three to four days to a couple of weeks.

When *thoroughly* dry, remove the pins and carding from the fins and tail. Inspect your work closely; brush off any dust or borax. If you have any split or damaged fins, you may repair them from the back side with a little clear mending tape held in place with any good clear household cement. One of my first students made a habit of saving fins and tails from his fishing catches to repair damaged areas in the fishes that he was mounting, sometimes replacing very large areas so cleverly that it was almost impossible to detect the repairs.

Now you are ready to paint your fish. You may use tube oil colors for this if you happen to have a set; they dry rather slowly, however, and I would recommend a set of the little bottled enamels that you can buy in most hobby shops. Use the color sparingly—thin it way down! If you don't, your fishes' markings will look glassy and faked. Too much color is worse than not enough. Follow your original color drawing very carefully. Use a bit of cotton on the end of a matchstick or toothpick to "blend" or subdue the shininess when you get too much on. Don't hesitate to clean off a wrong color with a little solvent and start over!

I generally begin by painting the light areas of the body first, working up to the darker portions of the back last. Another neat wrinkle that one of my students found was that some automotive spray paints were almost identical in color to the natural metallic colors on some of his fish, and he used these very effectively. I make good use of pearl essence, which I spray on the bellies of my fish. As a matter of fact, I use an airbrush on most of my specimens, but very good work can be done with brushes and a lot of thought and experimentation. Do *not* try to paint lacquers *over* enamel or oils! They will wrinkle your paint job every time.

When you have finished your colors, you can "mist" a finish coat of clear spray varnish or plastic over your entire fish. This will give it that "wet" look and help to protect it from accumulations of dust.

With this completed, you may now remove your fish from its temporary panel and place it on any finished panel that you desire. A screw eye in the middle of the back of this will now complete your work, and you may hang your trophy on the wall: *completed!*

As I said at the beginning of this lesson, you should expect to reach this point with a degree of success directly proportionate to the care that you have used in your work and the faithfulness with which you have followed these instructions. Do not be disappointed if it is not perfect. . . . Try another one. *Practice* will bring you closer to that "perfect" one.

Have fun and good luck!

PART II

Heads It Is

HEADS IT IS

Most fishermen are "head savers" of one sort or another—note the sightless totems with mouths wide-spread that line the posts and docks of every fishing spot in the state; or go into the garage of any fisherman and look over his assortment of yellowed, sun-dried, oily little trophies. He had to clean 'em anyway—had to remove the heads—so it was only a logical follow-up to spread the gill covers to their widest extremity and with a couple of shingle nails secure him to a post or stud. This operation was then completed with a plug of wood or clothespin wedged between the jaws to hold them firmly in place until the rays of the sun had locked the whole into one leathery, fiddle-brown countenance.

Needless to say, most of these efforts are not exactly attractive. Their sunken eyes, hollow cheeks, and general oily appearance do not appeal to most housewives. The fisherman may have notions of giving it a couple of coats of varnish or shellac in hopes of smothering that dried-fish odor; if it's the head of a real lunker, he "really" plans on finishing it up someday, but in the meantime it is relegated to its place on the post, and there it will probably stay.

For each of those who have such a garage or dock collection, there is the counterpartner who got a real nice pike or musky on that summer trip "up North." He still has the head in the deep freeze and plans to have it mounted someday; it isn't really such a big job and couldn't cost too awfully much, but in the meantime, there it too will stay.

It's for these two groups of people that I am writing this section of this little book. Really, it *isn't* such a big job! It doesn't require any great artistic ability! A fish's head does a fairly good job of holding its shape even when dried in the sun. Sooner or later, that head has to come out of the freezer . . . why not now?

Let's say that the specimen at hand is a ten- or twelve-pound pike or musky—or maybe a seven-pound bass, either freshly caught or frozen. The nicest heads when they are completed are those that include a portion of the shoulder with the pectoral fins spread fanlike onto the shield or plaque on which it is mounted. This calls for a

little advance planning when cleaning that fish; a little of the meat is sacrificed, but no great amount. Instead of cutting the head off at the upper part of the gill opening, cut it off an inch or so *behind* the gills, as shown by the dotted line in Plate 15.

This is very easily done by using a sharp butcher-knife on any but the largest fish. The vertebrae can easily be cut through with a small

PLATE 15

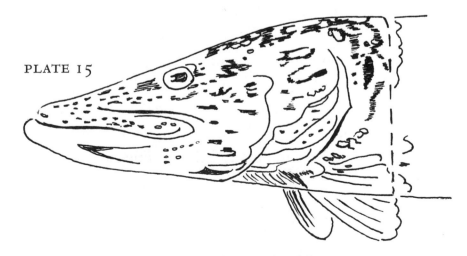

keyhole saw or in many cases with a coarse-toothed hacksaw. I suggest that you be liberal with the amount of body skin left on the head portion—many of the scales will "pop" out as you make this incision. If you are skimpy at this point, you may wind up your efforts with several scales obviously missing. As you will later understand, this skin will not be folded over the back of the head form, but will be tacked to the *edge*. Any excess of skin will later be clipped off using a pair of shears or tin snips. This will provide an edge that will snugly butt up to the plaque on which your finished head will be mounted.

Your next step will be to make two drawings of your fish head. Both are contact drawings, made by tracing around the outlines of your fish, just as was directed in the first section of this book. Since *both* sides of the head will show, place either side down on a large piece of paper, and holding a pencil perpendicular to the paper, follow the profile of the fish, making an accurate, contour drawing of him. (See Plate 16.) It is well to prop the mouth open in about the position desired at this point, for an open mouth will not give you the same contour as a closed one.

After completing this drawing, place the shoulders of your fish on the paper and make an accurate drawing of his cross section, as in Plate 16B. (You may protect your paper by covering the severed flesh with a swatch of waxed paper.) As you make this drawing, lift the head slightly with your free hand to ease the weight that will be pressing down on your paper, as this will tend to "flatten" and distort your drawing. You want this to be as near to lifelike as you can make it. Your two finished drawings should look somewhat like Plate 16A and Plate 16B.

It is wise at this time to make whatever color notes you deem necessary to help you in restoring those colors when your trophy is in a stage of completion. (Basically, the mounting of a head involves the same problems as were outlined in the mounting of smaller fish.)

PLATE 16

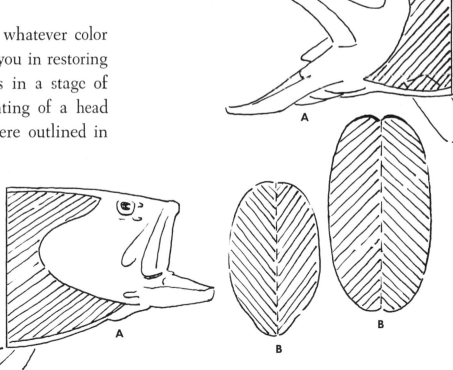

You are now ready to put your drawings aside and get at the task of skinning. If your specimen has not been thoroughly washed, now is the time to do this. If it is a pike, pickerel, or musky, you will find a great deal of "slime" or mucus covering him that makes for mighty slippery handling—even dangerous, as those teeth are razor sharp, as any old taxidermist or fisherman can testify. A wadding of newspaper crammed into the mouth while skinning the head will save you some nasty cuts from those teeth. It will also provide a more secure grip on an otherwise "handleless" head.

Use plenty of water—a good stiff paintbrush is a great help. Some common table salt sprinkled liberally as you wash the insides of the mouth, teeth, and tongue will greatly facilitate the removal of this troublesome coating.

Now, before you go any farther with this book *and* your fish, take time to really examine that fish! Sure, it's all right to read what I have written and examine my drawings, but much of what I say and attempt to show you will be absolutely lost unless you are well oriented as regards your own fish. I have used several different specimens in making these drawings, but, generally speaking, what applies to one applies to all.

Feel the cheeks and jaws of your fish with your fingers—this will often give you a clue as to an area of underlying flesh that will need some special attention. True, the Formalin-borax solution will "get at" and preserve almost any minor scraps of fleshy or cartilaginous tissue, but it will not altogether stop the shrinkage of such tissue or

PLATE 17

The unskinned head

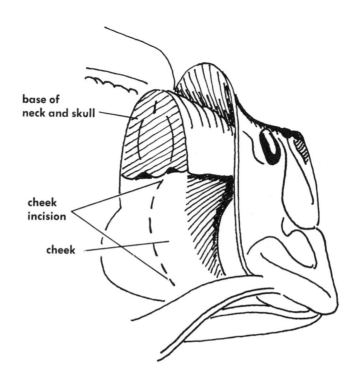

base of
neck and skull

cheek
incision

cheek

the later discoloration of your trophy brought on by the seepage of those "oils" that have been left in any quantity in those fleshy areas.

As you plan your approach with your fish and these drawings before you, keep in mind that a fish—unlike a bird or mammal—has no feathers or fur to hide any incision that you will be forced to make. Therefore, you will see the necessity of making as *few* cuts as possible and in such areas as will not be visible when your job is finished! Fortunately, this is relatively simple: Make *all* the cuts from the open back side of your fish.

(Incidentally, if you are seriously interested in continuing your work to large entire fish, keep all of this material in mind, for it will apply in exactly the same fashion to those fish.)

Plate 17 shows the inside of the left cheek of this bass, along with a dotted line representing the incision through which you reach the "pocket" of flesh indicated by the dotted line in Plate 20. After the incision has been made with your scissors, this little pocket can be cleaned out very effectively with a hook fashioned from a piece of a coat hanger. This hook should be smoothed off so that there are no sharp corners that might otherwise tear the exterior skin. You will shortly learn that much of your "seeing" in these areas will actually be done with your fingers. As you support the head with one hand and probe through the incision with the other, you will be able to feel the hard metal hook as it approaches the exterior skin through the muscle. Use reasonable care in this and you will experience no great difficulty.

Plate 17 also shows the base of the neck and skull, which can be removed with your scissors and diagonal cutters. The bony portion of vertebrae can be crushed and dragged forth with a pair of pliers. This tissue will *not* come out in a nice clean lump! It is tightly interlaced with the bony portion of the skull, and all is firmly attached to the skin. Leave enough of this "hard" tissue to allow the skin to retain its shape.

At this time, it may be well to mention that once a fish has been "roughed out" it is really helpful to submerge the entire head in your borax-Formalin solution for a few hours. You will find that this will toughen the skin and sort of "rubberize" the otherwise slippery fleshy scraps. These then can be picked and scraped loose quite easily (*with care*).

It is a good idea to have your container of borax-Formalin solution mixed up and ready to receive your fish head before beginning your skinning operation. Keep the recipe in mind so that you won't have to be constantly referring to it:

For *each* quart of water, add one handful of 20-Mule Team borax; stir; add one liberal eyedropper of 37 per cent USP formaldehyde.

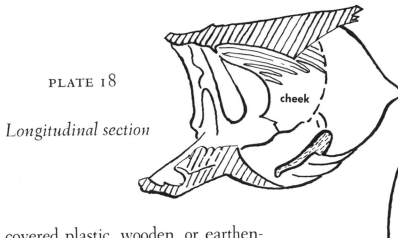

PLATE 18

Longitudinal section

Keep in a covered plastic, wooden, or earthen-
ware container. If for any reason your work is
interrupted—whether for a few hours, or days—
just plunk the old head into this until you can get
back to it.

Remember: Formaldehyde is caustic and poisonous. Don't use a metal container, and keep out
of the reach of children!

If you are having any difficulty in "seeing" the
interior portion of the head as I describe it, take a
look at Plates 18, 19, 20, and 21. Plate 19 shows
essentially the same view as Plate 21—that is, looking into the head from behind through the spread
pectoral girdle and gill covers. Plate 19 has *not*
had anything removed. Again, the dotted lines
represent the incisions in the *back* of the cheeks.

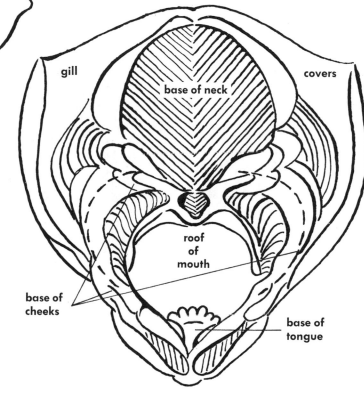

PLATE 19

Looking into the head from behind
(unskinned)

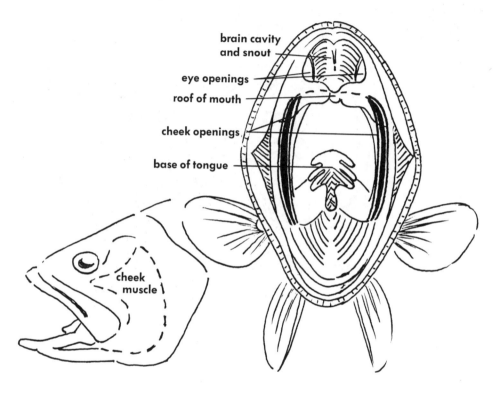

brain cavity
and snout

eye openings

roof of mouth

cheek openings

base of tongue

cheek
muscle

PLATE 20   PLATE 21

*The cleaned head
(from behind)*

Because this is difficult to visualize, I cut this head in half (see Plate 18) to better show this trouble spot of flesh and how to reach it.

Plate 21, looking directly into the fish's mouth from *behind,* shows the brain case removed. The eyes, too, have been taken from their sockets, allowing the eye openings to be visible. The base of the tongue has been cleaned up with the scissors; the gills have also been clipped out neatly, and the muscles from the cheeks have been removed from the two openings shown.

Most of this business of skinning your fish head has been accomplished with a minimum of tools: knife, scissors, diagonal cutters, pliers, and a key-hole saw. Except for the saw, you will have little further need for these tools and may put them away preparatory to making an artificial head for your trophy. In the meantime, place the head in your container of borax-Formalin solution. Be sure it is completely submerged, and agitate it about every few hours to make sure there are no "air pockets" and that the solution reaches all areas uniformly.

As was mentioned in Part I on the treatment of smaller fish, this solution has a solidifying action on the tissues, so be sure you have the jaws opened in the position desired; otherwise you will have difficulty in changing them. For the same reason, "arrange" and block the gill covers in as natural an attitude as you can. *Do not* leave it cramped or distorted in any way expecting to correct it later, or you will surely be disappointed. You will learn

from experience that convenient pieces of scrap wood such as a broken yardstick will greatly assist you in "propping" such areas as the gills and jaws.

If it happens that you have a very large head with a lot of cheek muscle removed, it is well to fill the cheek "pouches" from behind with cotton or paper toweling, which will later be removed. Don't bulge them, as though he's blowing a trumpet; just keep him as natural as possible. Now, with all of this accomplished, you may put him in his tank for as long as you wish (or over twelve hours) while you turn your efforts to the artificial headform.

Looking back to your two contact drawings of the fish (see Plate 16), you will now make a set of patterns for the two pieces of wood on which you will base the headform. The shaded portion of Plate 16 indicates roughly the shape of each of these two pieces. Only your own knowledge of the amount of bony material you left in your fish can tell you how much smaller you should make the form than the contour drawing you made. It is better to make it slightly *under*size than to make it too big and later have to make it over. Any deficiency that you have may be filled in later with papier-mâché, when you are actually installing it in the skin. Keep in mind that at all stages of producing this headform, it's a good idea to "try it on for size" frequently. Don't blunder ahead and find out too late that you made it too big!

Depending on the kind of tools that are avail-able to you—whether a keyhole, saber, jig, cop-ing, or band saw (even a pocketknife)—cut these two pieces out of whatever soft wood is available. Pine, poplar, willow, gum, or fir are as good as any. Hardwoods too, are all right, but they pre-sent difficulties in their harder-working qualities. The wood should be of about three-quarter-inch thickness.

After cutting these pieces and determining that they will fit the skin, they may be screwed to-gether with a couple of flat-head wood screws about 1½ inches long—countersunk on the back, as shown in Plates 22 and 23. Just make sure that it forms a good *solid* frame, as you will later pound nails into its edge, and it must be strong enough to support the completed head.

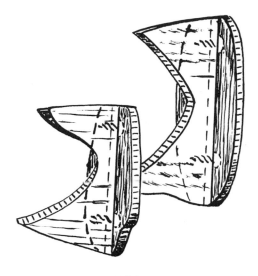

PLATE 22

The wooden form

While you still have your woodworking tools out, this is a good time to prepare a temporary mounting board, as shown in Plate 25. You may use a piece of plywood or composition building board, such as is commonly used for subsiding or insulation. It should be at least three or four inches larger in every direction than the base of

PLATE 23

*"Foam" blocks
in place*

PLATE 24

The formed head

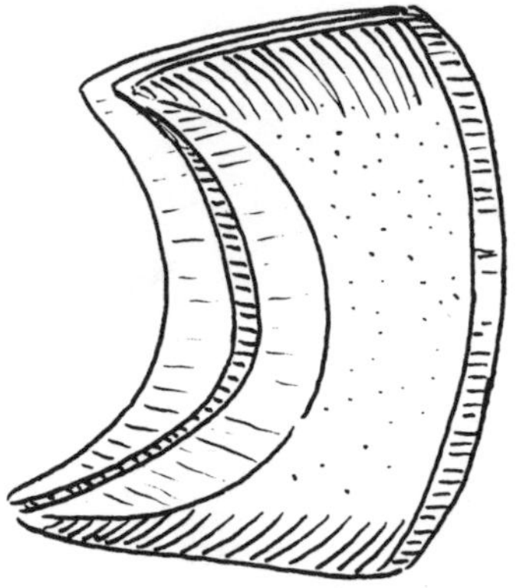

your fish. This will give you adequate space on which to spread the fins and gill covers. Center the headform on the mounting board, and bore two holes through the board. The holes must correspond to the holes you will necessarily bore in the ends of your headform. Then fasten the headform to the mounting board with wood screws inserted from the back of the mounting board.

Now select two pieces of urethane foam—or any "foam" material that you have determined will not be affected by solvents or oils—in most cases, not over two inches thick and large enough to glue into position, as I have shown in Plate 23. If some other material such as balsa wood is available, it will work just as well; just use a little common sense in regard to all you do, and you

won't go wrong. (If you need additional thickness, glue two or more pieces together with any good glue.)

After giving the glue ample time to dry—generally overnight—get out that good sharp knife I suggested in Part I and "rough out" your artificial head. Use some sandpaper to finish it up so that it will look somewhat like the drawing in Plate 24.

Now try the skin on it. If it fits fairly well, fine! If it does not, remove it and make whatever corrections are necessary. With this completed, you are ready to pose the skin over the form and secure it firmly in place.

Most taxidermists use a good form of paste or glue when "mounting" hides or skins on their artificial forms. This greatly facilitates the moving and adjusting that are necessary on most large specimens. When mounting large entire fish, this is especially desirable, as the glue certainly holds the skin firmly in place when it is dry. If you have been around such studios, you may have observed quite a variety of these adhesives: casein, dextrin, linoleum paste, and even library paste, to mention a few. A fish's head, however, is quite bony, and with reasonable care in fashioning the head-form, you should need none of these. The little nails that you will use around the edge as shown in Plate 25 will suffice.

Remove your specimen from its borax-Formalin bath and rinse it well in clean water. Check it carefully for any loose bits of clinging flesh that should be picked or scraped off. Now try it

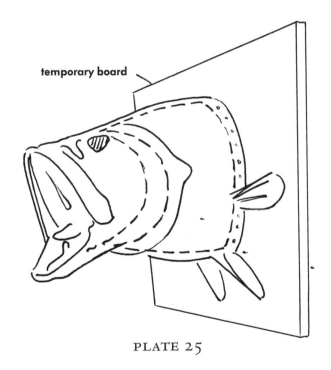

temporary board

PLATE 25

Form in place, temporary board

on the headform again just to make sure it will fit properly. If it does and you are satisfied with it, remove the skin from its form and, reaching into the cheeks from behind with a pair of tweezers, remove the cotton or paper "stuffing" that filled the cheeks while the fish was in the solution. You will now replace this with papier-mâché backed up with a fresh wadding of cotton or soft paper.

(A word of advice at this point: Commercial papier-mâché "sets up" in a relatively short time, generally about one-half hour. Be sure that you are ready to "model" it shortly after placing it in position.)

In mixing your mâché, use the dry, powdered form that may be purchased cheaply from any taxidermist's supply house (generally for less than $.20 per pound). It does a much smoother job than the homemade variety. Until you learn not to waste it, make a guess at the quantity you will need for the cheeks and any unwanted cavities that will need filling in your mount. Place the dry powder in a shallow pie pan. Add a little cold water gradually as you mix it with a spatula or table knife; use only enough water to bring it to a smooth "putty like" consistency. Lay a smooth lump of this mâché in the cheeks—through the opening in the back—and follow it with a swatch of fresh cotton or soft paper tissue to provide a "cork" through which the moisture can escape during the drying process. Model the cheeks somewhat from the outside to assure yourself that you have an amount sufficient to do the job, but not enough to make the cheeks bulge.

Now add enough mâché to the surface of your headform to insure a nice snug fit in all places. Press a small ball of mâché into the fin butts to be later modeled and shaped to the head. Immediately slip the head into place in the skin and adjust it to its proper position. Be sure the mouth plug is in position so that it will require no further changing of the jaws. *Again, check the cheeks* for smoothness and uniformity.

Using brass banker's pins or escutcheon nails, tack around the base of the head into the wooden base board. Space the pins close enough together to assure a nice smooth fit. Do *not* drive them all the way in as you will later clip off the heads so that they will not show. Start your nailing at the top of the head, then the throat, then alternate one nail on either side until the head is secure.

Upon completion of your tacking, check the head carefully to see that none of your mâché has been dislodged or distorted. Since you will have already placed a quantity of mâché in the base of the fin butts, you should now "card" and spread the fins before the mâché has had a chance to "set."

Place your fish in position on your temporary mounting board, and secure it there with two No. 8 or No. 9 flat-head wood screws about 1½ inches long. Using pieces of waxed (so the fins won't stick) cardboard, cut slightly larger than each fin, spread and secure each fin to the temporary board, as in Plate 26. Use ordinary straight pins or banker's pins for this.

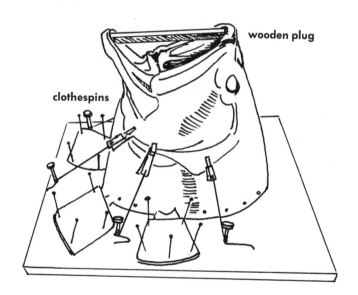

wooden plug

clothespins

PLATE 26

The fins carded

Give your attention now to the gill covers. These will ordinarily creep together accordion-like and must be held separate while drying if you wish to show anything of the gills. Small plastic clothespins work very well for this purpose. Tie a piece of string to each one before attaching it to the gill covers. This will then give you a means of anchoring these pins securely to nails that you will place strategically around your fish. After the fish has dried, these spread features will maintain their position permanently. (See Plate 26.)

At this stage, you may relax somewhat, as drying takes considerable time. At any time during this drying period you may mix up fresh lumps of mâché with which to set the eyes in place, finish the inside of the mouth, and rebuild the portion of the gills that will be exposed.

With the main portion of your labors behind you, your "finishing touches" are just as important as every step that preceded them; *don't* skimp on them. Finish the interior of the open mouth while the skin is drying so that it will all dry together.

You will soon discover that the drying skin will shrink somewhat; also, that the mâché does too. As this happens, mix fresh mâché and fill the cracks as they appear. Your first application to the interior of the mouth and gullet should be made within a day or two of the actual mounting of the skin.

Preparatory to modeling the fish's mouth, cut

a piece of thin cardboard roughly the shape of the back of the fish's gullet. Press this snugly against the temporary mounting board on the inside of the mouth. This will serve as a "dike" and separator so that your head will not stick tightly to the board when you are ready to remove it as you place it on a permanent plaque.

Now drop a healthy chunk of the mâché into the back of the mouth against this cardboard dike. Using your fingers, smooth this lump out, "blending" it into the hardening edges of the skin of the tongue, roof, cheeks, and throat. Let this harden and dry for two or three days, then add enough fresh mâché to allow you to *carefully* model all the details that are necessary to please you.

The open gills may be treated in exactly the

same way—and at the same time. Many devices may be used to recreate these structures. Pieces of cardboard, fiberboard, or sheet plastic can be inserted in the moist mâché to give a very realistic quality to your work. Some very expert taxidermists simply leave the real gills attached to the skin as it goes through the borax-Formalin bath, and the gills are then "carded" in the same manner as the fins. I prefer to model them from the moist mâché. Your experimentation will soon lead you to a method of your own.

Now for the eyes. Generally the small-to-medium sizes will come from the supply houses attached to a small wire. Some will be smooth on the back. Either one can be "set" directly into the eye socket on a bedding of mâché, and the mâché's adhesive quality is all that is necessary to hold the eyes firmly in place. If the eyes do have a wire, clip off all but about one-half inch or so to be imbedded in the mâché.

Eye color, too, is an important item to consider. Eyes may be purchased prepainted for specific species, or they may be secured with only the pupil imbedded in the glass for you to paint as you wish on the smooth back side. These are generally referred to as "flint" eyes and are considerably cheaper than the painted ones. Unless you are more of a stickler for detail than the average person, you will be well pleased with the painted ones, and the few cents' difference in cost will soon be forgotten.

Eyes, by the way, are measured in millimeters

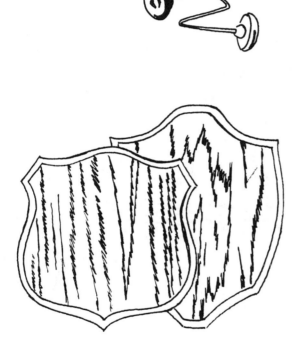

PLATE 27

*Typical glass eyes
and plaques*

and cost from about $.20 per pair for the smallest to about $2.00 per pair for the 22mm size.

With the eyes now set, the interior of the mouth and the gills modeled, and all little shrinkage cracks filled, you are ready to set the mounted head aside to dry *completely*. This may require as much as three or four weeks or as little as three or four days, depending upon drying conditions and the size of the head.

When it is completely dry, remove all "carding," pins, and strings from your fish and prepare to paint it exactly as was described in Part I of this book. Clip the heads from the nails that secure the skin to its headform and smooth up the nails with a file so that they may be painted over and hidden. If you choose to use any kind of spray paints or varnishes, it is a good idea to "wipe" a film of Vaseline with your fingertip over the surface of the glass eyes. Then when you have finished painting your fish, any paint or varnish will readily be removed with a little rubbing.

Remove the head from its temporary mounting board and secure an appropriate hanger to the back of a prefinished plaque—whether your own design or "store-bought"—and you are ready for it to receive your finished fish. This should be secured with the same screws that held it to its temporary mounting board.

If you have followed these instructions, you will have a trophy that should certainly be a pleasure to you and will probably even outlast you!

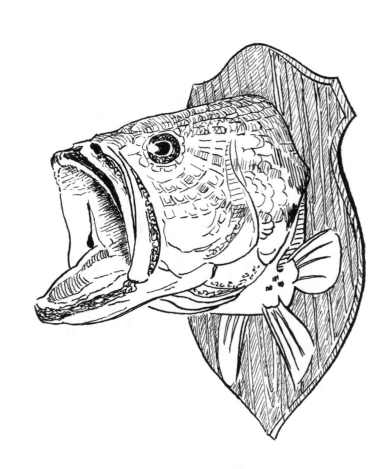

PLATE 28

The finished head

PART III

The Big Ones

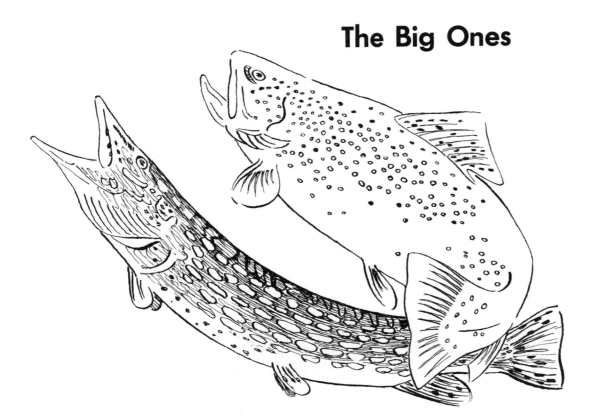

A few months ago, a young man came to me with a beautiful large-mouth bass that he had "mounted." I *should* say that he had "stuffed"—for that was the case—and he was in big trouble! He had taken some taxidermy lessons through a correspondence course and had undertaken this job for a friend who wanted to save the expense of having his fish mounted by an experienced taxidermist.

It was obvious that the young man had good natural abilities, for he had done a beautiful job of skinning and of painting his fish; had he known more about his basic materials, I'm sure that he would have done the job very adequately. Where he *had* gone wrong was that he had actually "stuffed" the skin with moist paper pulp, mis-takenly thinking of it as papier-mâché! Now, inside that almost waterproof skin—with almost no means for moisture to escape—he had a heavy, soggy mass that could not possibly "harden"—and, as it did dry out somewhat, it shrank away from his fish, leaving unwanted hollows and depressions.

By removing the paint from his fish with lacquer thinner and opening it up to remove the pulp, we did manage to save his fish and re-mounted it on a foam body such as I am about to describe. The boy was saved the embarrassment of a ruined fish, and he certainly learned something in the process. This is but one of the problems that are certain to be encountered with any "stuffing" process and why I shall not enter into any description of that ancient technique. Even had the boy used a regular mixture of mâché—which would have hardened—he would still have had a mount that would have taken weeks to dry and would have been as heavy as lead! Enough said on that subject.

Now, if you have mounted a few smaller fish and enjoyed a measure of success, it's only a matter of time until you or one of your friends will get a real "lunker" and you will be unable to restrain yourself from trying that too. From past experience, I know that once your fishermen buddies get a glimpse of some of your mounts, you will have all the fish to mount that you care to do.

While the steps involved with these larger fish are basically the same as for smaller ones, there are some guides that will give you assurance that you will not spoil that first really nice trophy. If you have mounted a few good-sized heads such as described in Part II, you will have very little trouble in moving on to these larger fish.

The one thing that generally hinders the novice is in the proper making of a superfitting, artificial body—one that gives the fish that bit of snap, that twist as he tries to throw a lure, that movement of body that makes the fisherman recall exactly how he looked when he first broke water!

This is the kind of action that you will want to put into your *big* fish—and this is especially true if you have any ideas of going into the business of fish taxidermy.

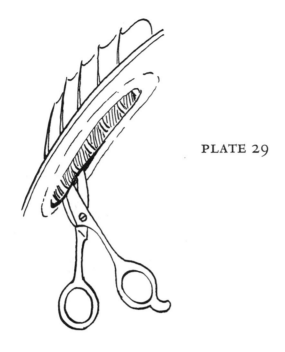

PLATE 29

Skinning the larger fish is exactly the same process that I described in Part I, with the addition of some extra attention to the base of the fins. These will be found to contain considerably more fleshy material that must be opened up, scraped clean, and prepared sufficiently for the action of the borax-Formalin solution. Largely, this can be done with the same scissors used in Parts I and II. Plate 29 shows you the area that I refer to. *Do not cut out the spines themselves*—just that fleshy area around them. The voids left between these will be filled with mâché just prior to adjusting the skin over the artificial body. Do this on each of the fins as well as the tail.

Another word of caution in this stage of skinning larger fish: Don't think for one minute that you can flop this big one around carelessly without losing some scales. They'll pop out as easily as on the smaller ones, and their absence will be a lot more noticeable! *Keep that skin flat on the table . . . and keep it wet!* If necessary, tape a sheet of plastic to the table to provide a slick surface, and refrain from scooting it around any more than necessary.

If you have a buddy (a wife will do nicely) to hold up the body as you clip under it with your

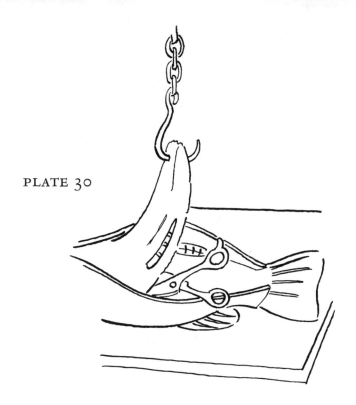

PLATE 30

scissors—great! If not, rig up an adjustable hook that can be raised as you need. (See Plate 30.)

If you find your scissors to be inadequate for some of the bone and spine clipping, use a small pair of tin snips or diagonal cutters. Most of the actual clipping, though, can be done with the scissors. Later, as you clean up the roughed-out skin, use a "shearing" motion to clean up the larger areas of clinging flesh around the fins, tail, head, and gill collar. An ordinary dinner teaspoon is a fine tool with which to scrape the final bits of fat and flesh from the interior of the skin. Just take it easy and you'll experience no great difficulty.

Upon completion of the "rough" skinning, it is helpful to submerge the skin in your tub of borax-

Formalin for a few hours. Try it—you'll find that the slippery quality of the fresh flesh will completely disappear, while the skin itself will be much toughened for your final cleanup.

Now with the skin safely in its tub, let's turn to the job of creating an accurate and lifelike body for your fish:

If you have a modicum of artistic ability and patience, you will be able to enlarge upon the instructions given in Part I for making an artificial body. I know from experience, though, that many do not have much of this ability. If you feel that you belong in this latter category, don't lose heart, friend, you can still do a very creditable job if you'll just follow either of the two methods following. I greatly prefer the use of the foam body, for it is more resilient when completed and in place in the skin. Fish skins shrink somewhat upon drying, some more than others; if the specimen is hung in a superheated area, such as above a hot-air register, I have known cases where beautiful trophies have literally burst open because the body on which they were mounted had no "give." Foam, and to a slightly lesser degree, laminated paper bodies, such as I will treat second, have this very desirable characteristic: They give.

I also give preference to the foam body because it is more direct in method and takes less time—*if* made correctly the first time. If you have to make two or three passes at it, however, you may save time by using the cast, laminated papier-mâché form. There certainly can be no argument with the fact that you will have a body that fits in this procedure. Try both methods and decide for yourself which method suits your abilities best.

The large foam body: If you were going to mount your fish in a perfectly flat attitude, such as is shown by the bass in Plate 32, you would have no problem. You would proceed just as you did in Part I. Where all beginners go astray is where they try to give their body that natural

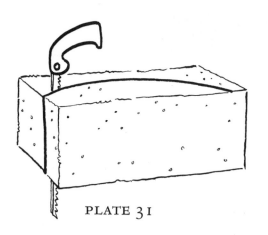

PLATE 31

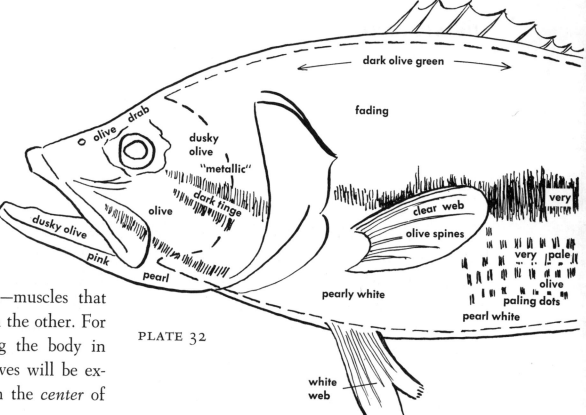

dark olive green

fading

olive drab

dusky olive

"metallic"

dark tinge

olive

dusky olive

pink

pearl

clear web

olive spines

very

very pale

olive

paling dots

pearly white

pearl white

PLATE 32

white web

twist or turn of the living fish—muscles that stretch on one side and contract on the other. For this reason, I recommend making the body in *two* pieces, individually. Both halves will be exactly the same shape *only* through the *center* of the fish.

Select a block of foam large enough to make the entire body. If necessary, glue two or more pieces together. Now decide on how much of a "curve" you intend to have on him when finished. With a crayon or soft pencil, mark this curve longitudinally on the block of foam, as you see in Plate 31.

Using a keyhole saw, cut through the entire block, following this line accurately. Use care in doing this, as you will later glue these two pieces back together. They must and will fit properly.

Now go back to the original contact drawing

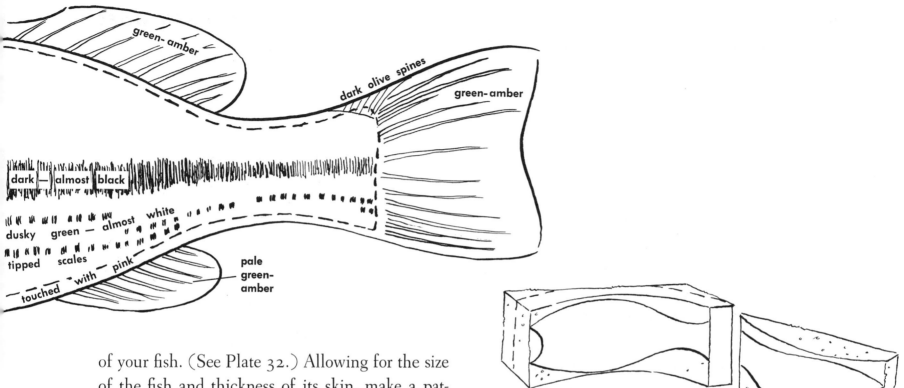

green-amber

dark olive spines

green-amber

dark — almost black

dusky green — almost white tipped scales
touched with pink

pale green-amber

PLATE 33

of your fish. (See Plate 32.) Allowing for the size of the fish and thickness of its skin, make a pattern on heavy wrapping paper as the dotted line indicates. Place this pattern on the *curved* surfaces of both pieces of foam, and draw around it on both pieces. Make sure the two drawings correspond accurately, as in Plate 33. With the keyhole saw, rough both of these out, just as you did in Part I.

Work on only one "half" at a time until you

have both pieces fairly well shaped. If you have kept the skinned body at hand, make frequent references to it for thickness and similarity. As it really begins to take on shape, hold the two halves firmly together as you complete it with a piece of coarse sandpaper. *Don't* alter the shape of your original pattern. If necessary, pin it to each half individually and work carefully to its edge. If you do this, you will make no mistakes; the only place you might go wrong will be in making it too thick or too thin.

When the two halves are completed to your satisfaction, you will need to glue a wooden block into the *back* half of the body. Predrill two holes in a block of soft wood to match suitably spaced screws in a temporary and final mounting panel, just the same as we did in Parts I and II. You may cut a suitable opening to fit this block of wood in the back half of the body by using a hacksaw blade, as in the top drawing of Plate 34.

With this block glued in place, glue the two

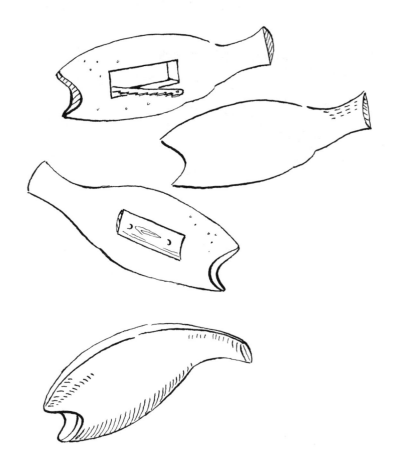

PLATE 34

halves together, just as the lower illustration shows in Plate 34. As soon as the glue sets, you are ready to "try on the skin." So much for the foam body. Now let's take a look at another method—one that I used for years before the advent of the "foams":

The laminated paper body: This method is especially well suited for very large fish—where it would be impractical to find blocks of foam large enough to do the job. It involves making a plaster mold of your fish *before* skinning it. If you already have some knowledge of mixing and pouring plaster of Paris, your task will be considerably simplified. If you have had no such experience, it would be well to mix and pour a small batch or two experimentally, for plaster generates heat upon "setting," and you don't want to keep a heated fish around any longer than absolutely necessary. If you do exactly as I say, you will have him in and out of his plaster shell within two hours—which won't hurt him a bit!

First: about that business of mixing plaster of Paris. Use No. 1 molding plaster, such as may be obtained from most building supply firms, generally at a cost of less than $5.00 per hundred-pound bag. Druggists sell a highly refined plaster under the name of "Dental Plaster," but at a much greater cost. Do not be confused by other gypsum products, such as wall or "patching" plaster; plaster of Paris is what you want.

Now about mixing it: Any plastic container will do well as a mixing vessel. Discarded plastic bleach bottles with the top cut off are as good as any—besides, you won't have to wash them when you're finished. *Never* wash *any* amount of plaster down the drain. (It will "set" even under water.) Another "never": Never start with more than one half of your container filled with water; by the time you've added the plaster, your container will overflow!

Here is a good rule of thumb to use for *any* quantity of plaster you wish to mix:

1. As in Plate 36, place whatever quantity of clean, cold water you wish in a suitable container.

2. Sprinkle in handsful of plaster of Paris until it floats rather uniformly on top of the water, making little "islands." Do *not* mix it at any time until you have added this quantity. Whether you

PLATE 35

PLATE 36

have mixed one pint or one gallon, this is the quantity of plaster necessary to mix properly and "set" quickly.

3. Mix this thoroughly with your hand or a paddle. Stir it until it is nice and creamy—about like melted ice cream. By trying a couple of small batches, you will learn to mix and stir it so that it will "set" within five minutes of being poured—this is what you want.

4. Shortly after the plaster "sets," you will notice it warming up considerably. Don't try to move a "hot" mold, as it will break. Let it cool before handling it.

5. If additional layers are necessary, they may be added at any time after the first batch has been poured. If you need to give extra strength to a very large mold, you may add strips of burlap dipped in your plaster along with pieces of wire or other reinforcement metal.

6. When you wish to cause two pieces of plaster to separate, as in this two-piece mold, coat the cold surfaces of the first piece with either bar or liquid soap before pouring the second half.

Now you know about plaster of Paris. Let's back up and prepare your fish for casting: As in Plate 35, make a shallow sandbox that will comfortably accommodate your fish. Borrow enough from the kids to fill your box a little over half full. Use slightly dampened sand so that it will "tamp" well. Scoop out a slight depression that will fit your fish, then raise his tail until it's in a natural attitude, and tamp sand under it. If his belly sags un-

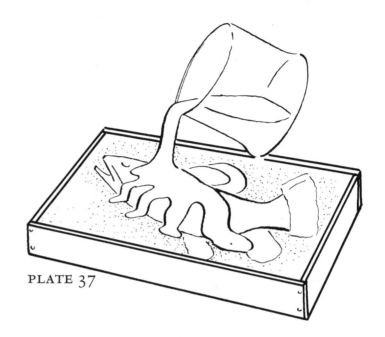

PLATE 37

attractively, shove some sand under it. Tamp the sand smoothly all the way around him until he is half buried. If your wife has tolerated all of this on her kitchen table, you will find that a butter knife and spoon are very good to do this tamping and smoothing with. (Incidentally, one of the greatest fish taxidermists I've ever known of was a housewife.)

Now that he is imbedded in the sand, tear pieces of toilet or facial tissue into suitable pieces to cover his fins, as in Plate 35. After it is in place, dampen it with water to hold it there. This is a precautionary measure to assure you that these will not become locked in the plaster and be damaged when it is removed. Stuff some wastepaper in his mouth and cover it with tissue for the same reason.

Next, mix a batch of plaster as directed. Just before it seems ready to "set," pour it gently over your fish, being careful not to dislodge your tissue paper protectors. (See Plate 37.) If additional layers of plaster are necessary, mix them and add to the first.

As soon as this mold cools, carefully lift it *and* the fish from its sand bed. Turn it over as in Plate 38. Brush the sand off the surface of the mold and your fish. Water will not harm the mold, so feel free to sponge any areas clean that need it.

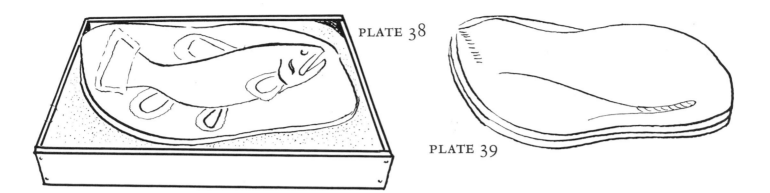

PLATE 38

PLATE 39

Now soap the exposed surface of the mold preparatory to pouring the second half. Use plenty of soap so that nothing will stick to the mold; a medium-sized paintbrush is good for this chore. Place tissue strips on the fins and mouth as you did on the other side, and you are ready to pour the second half. You may scoop sand around the edge of the mold to create a dike to contain the second layer.

Now mix and pour the second half, as you see has been done in Plate 39. When this has cooled, slip that butter knife into the soapy slit between the two halves and pry the two apart. Remove your fish gently from the mold and rinse him well in *cold* water. He will have picked up a little heat, but not enough to harm him if he was fresh

when you started. Plate 40 shows the two halves now with the fish removed. Lay these aside while you go about the business of skinning your fish, cleaning him, and immersing him in his borax-Formalin tub.

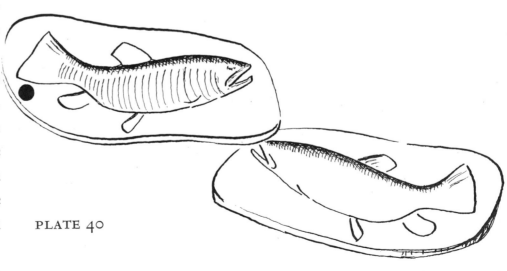

PLATE 40

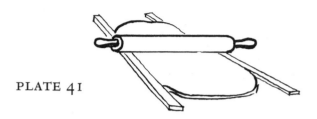

PLATE 41

(Incidentally, if a fish is in any stage of decomposition, the only thing you can do is to get him skinned and into the borax-Formalin solution as quickly as possible. Until you have attained some skill, don't even mess with any but a *fresh* one!)

With the fish skin out of the way, you may return to the job of making a laminated paper body: You have an accurate mold of the *outside* of your fish. From this, you must now subtract by one means or another an amount of your mold equivalent to the thickness of the skin—generally a layer about three-sixteenths or one-quarter inch in thickness. Relying again upon your wife's kitchen paraphernalia, this is relatively simple. Look at Plate 41 and you'll see what I mean. Instead of rolling out a pie crust—which I am sure

would work equally as well—we'll roll out a piece of potter's clay between two slats of wood to keep it of uniform thickness. A piece of broom would work as well as the rolling pin, but whatever you use, try to keep the clay as nearly the thickness of the skin as you can.

Potter's clay is the kind that comes from the earth and is moistened with water. It's the material that bricks, tile, and ceramicware are made of and can be bought from many builder's supply companies. Before you attempt to roll it out, it should be of such moistness that it will not stick to your hands, nor dry enough to crack when you bend it. Pat out a big chunk on a wrinkle-free dish towel so that you'll have something to pick it up by. Place your thickness sticks on each

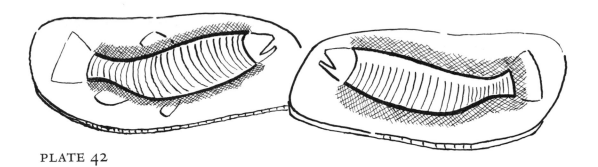

PLATE 42

side, and roll it out with a *dry* rolling pin. (If the pin is wet, the clay will stick to it.) Lift this layer of clay by the cloth and carefully press it into both halves of your mold, as indicated by the heavy lines in Plate 42. Smooth it out and trim it up with a spoon or knife.

Now place a large piece of cheesecloth over the clay in both halves. Let it extend over the edges of the molds for two or three inches all the way around. (See the cross-hatching in Plate 42.) Press it down snugly against the clay "skin." This will also become a "handle" when you remove the finished forms and will serve as a flap when you paste the two halves together.

For the actual laminations of paper, you may use any paper that is tough, but not too stiff to shape well. Use two colors so that you can readily keep track of each complete layer. Building paper alternated with brown wrapping paper works very well. *Tear* it—rather than cut it—so the edges will blend softly into each other, into strips about one inch in width and as long as will lie smoothly with no wrinkles in your mold. Alternate each layer so that they will "crisscross" each other. Any good heavy-bodied paste will do for this: school paste, wheat-flour paste, or even linoleum paste will work. Just be sure that it isn't too wet, as you'll want it to dry out in reasonable time. A little drying between layers is a good idea. Five or six good solid layers are sufficient for most jobs. More may be necessary for very large ones.

Midway through your laminations on the

"back" half, stoutly secure a piece of wood between the layers of paper, as shown in Plate 43. This will assure you of a firm anchor when you fasten the finished fish to a panel.

Let the two halves dry now for several hours, until they have strength enough to be lifted from their molds. Before doing this, mark the edges carefully for any trimming that might be necessary. When they can be safely lifted and trimmed, place them back to back and securely paste the cheesecloth flaps to lock the *two* into *one*.

After the form has dried thoroughly, it should be sanded lightly and given a couple of coats of shellac to waterproof it, and then it's ready for use—a strong, lightweight form, as shown in Plate 44.

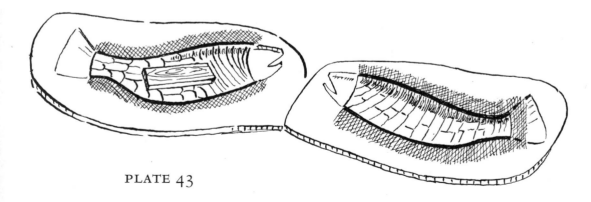

PLATE 43

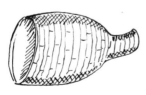

PLATE 44

Sound like a lot of work? It *is!* I only recommend it if you have found the foam method to be too much for you. It *is* a good, proven method that does give you a very accurate body for your fish.

Now, with a well-made artificial body at hand and your fish skin made ready, rinse the skin well in cold water and try the two together. Don't panic if you find the skin doesn't want to slip perfectly into place the first time; a large skin wants to "drag" over the dry body and has to be helped into position. You'll find that when this dry body is coated with paste, it will move much more freely into position. Right now, be content with making certain that the incision of the back will close up perfectly with no overlap. If you've done your work well, it will. Whatever you do, keep a cool head—and *don't* try to stretch the skin! (It will tear every time.) If the body is a little too small, build it up a little with papier-mâché. If it's a little too large, sand it down to size. My guess is that if you have been careful in following these instructions, your body will fit the first time. One further word of advice: Be sure the body is correctly placed fore and aft! A half inch too far one way or the other will throw you off completely.

After you've made sure that all is reasonably in order, remove the skin and *heavily* coat the body with paste. If you get too much on, it will only squoosh out the incision in the back, where it can be wiped off. Now lay a good lump of mâché up into the head and another thumb-sized bead of maché pressed well up into the fin butts and tail. Have it fairly soft so that it can be shaped easily from outside the skin.

Thrust the body into the head first, then adjust the skin along the back to the tail. Although a "handle" may be attached to the body so that it may be locked in a vise giving you two free hands to work with, I prefer to hold the body in one hand as I adjust the skin with the other. Pull the belly skin down and under until you have all the skin fairly in place. Hold it there with three or four large rubber bands until all adjusting is complete; then, beginning at the tail, staple the incision together using one-half or nine-sixteenths-inch pointed staples spaced one or two inches

apart. As you complete the incision and find that all is as it should be, go back over the incision and add whatever staples are necessary to hold the entire incision closed.

Now turn your fish over on the temporary mounting board, secure him there with two screws, and immediately model whatever maché you have used in the head, fins, and tail before it has a chance to "set." If you recall the "head work" of Part II, you will have no difficulty with any of this.

From here on, the carding of the fins, gills, and tail, and the drying, setting of eyes, painting, and final mounting on a panel are exactly the same procedures as were used in Parts I and II.

And now, friend, it's up to you.

TROUBLESHOOTERS' GUIDE

1. There are taxidermy supply companies that will furnish you with the eyes, foam (plastic), papier-mâché, etc., needed for your fish. Two such firms are: Van Dyke's, Woonsocket, South Dakota 57385; and Jonas Bros., Inc., 1037 Broadway, Denver, Colorado 80203

2. Large fish skins should remain in the borax-Formalin solution *at least* eighteen hours. Any amount of time *over* that will do the skin no harm.

3. You may speed up the setting time of plaster by adding a little salt to the water before mixing it.

4. For some reason, you may prefer to sew up your fish rather than staple it. It's much slower, but it's certainly acceptable.

5. It requires about one hour to skin a nice bass carefully. Don't worry if your first one takes much longer. It takes much longer to clean up the skin and head than it does to remove it.

6. You can buy ready-made plastic bodies. I have never used them, but have no doubt that they could be made to fit and would be all right.

7. Mount a catfish, spoonbill, or sturgeon *before* you do one for hire. Have plenty of aspirin on hand.

8. Be sure you wash the mucus from your fish *before* placing it in the borax-Formalin solution.

9. Repairing fins and tail: A few weeks ago, I had occasion to mount a large musky that had

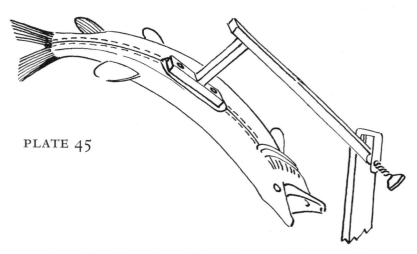

PLATE 45

badly damaged fins and tail—probably one quarter of the tail was gone. After completing the mounting and just prior to touching up the colors, I repaired these areas very effectively with Fiberglas matt and polyester resin as follows:

Use a temporary handle attached to the back of the fish. (See Plate 45.) Clamp the handle to your bench so that the entire back side is free and readily adjustable horizontally so that your resin will not trickle away from the areas of repair, as in this drawing.

Any commercial matt and resin will do. It's generally available as a patch or repair material for boats and autos and may be obtained at most large paint and repair stores at a reasonable cost. Directions for mixing the resin and its companion catalyst (hardener) will differ according to the brand, so it would be well to familiarize yourself with the brand available in your area before trying it on a nice specimen. Experiment a little. I use a "hotter" mix than generally specified to speed up the setting time; however, you must use care not to have it so "hot" that it will burn your work.

There are also some "casting plastics" on the market today that work equally as well with the Fiberglas matt. I prefer the matt to Fiberglas cloth because it blends much better with the existing scales and fins. When applied carefully, there will be no surface indication to show where the patch leaves off and the skin begins—a very desirable effect.

Clip out a piece of matt to use as a patch, slightly larger than the entire tail, as in the top drawing in Plate 46. Lay this aside while you prepare your resin, which generally amounts to adding a few drops of catalyst to the resin and stirring it thoroughly. Using a stiff brush, apply a liberal coating over the entire tail, then lay the patch in it and saturate the patch thoroughly with a good layer of the resin. Use a "dabbing" motion with your brush so as not to "bunch" or dislodge the fibers in the matt. You want the patch to be as uniform in thickness as you can get it.

As the matt is saturated, you will notice that it will change from white to almost transparent clearness. You want a complete penetration of the resin so that the crisscrossed fibers will not be apparent when you've finished. Additional layers may be added as you go along if they are necessary. (Clean your brush out immediately with lacquer thinner.)

By feeling the patch with your finger as it begins to "gel" or "set," you can determine when it reaches a leathery hardness. At this stage, you may trim it to shape with a razor blade. If the patch gets away from you and becomes brittle, you can do the same job with your skinning scissors and then smooth it up with a little sandpaper.

Now turn the fish over and give your atten-

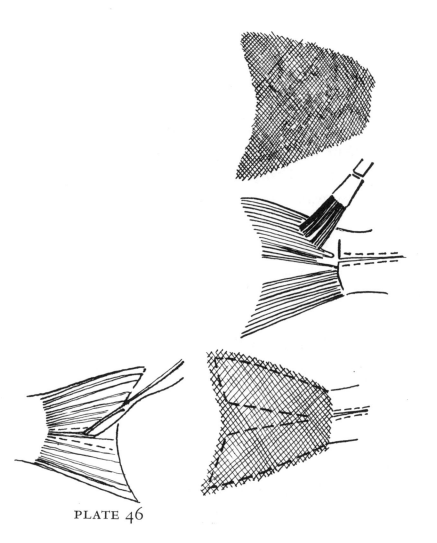

PLATE 46

tion to the front side of your patch. You'll notice that the resin is quite glossy and too slick to look natural, even though the patch is well formed. To remedy this, make a modeling material now with which to re-create the missing spines and web.

Take a small portion of your dry papier-mâché and mix it thoroughly with enough of your resin to make a rather heavy slurry. That's right—*just* the resin and the mâché. This will make a "gunk" type of material that *will not harden* until you add the catalyst as you need it. Now mix a small portion of this "gunk" with a few drops of the catalyst and immediately trowel it over the *front* side of the patch. As it begins to "gel," use an appropriate modeling tool to carefully shape and draw out the natural form of the missing spines, as in the bottom drawing in Plate 46. Sounds like a lot of bother? Sure, but it does a good job and is easily painted over.

This same technique can be applied to all the fins, and it certainly makes them endure the ravages of handling and dusting. However, it's easy to get carried away with too much trimming and "backing" and wind up with a fish that has fins that are so perfectly formed that it looks "fakey." I greatly prefer them to look as natural as I can make them, and this may include a few ragged edges.

10. Some of my students questioned me this summer about my instructions for the borax solution: a "handful" of borax and a "squirt" of form-aldehyde. Technically, what you want is a saturate solution of borax—that is, all that a given quantity of water will take up and *hold*. Anything more than that will not harm a thing. Borax is cheap, and that's why I advise a liberal handful.

As for the Formalin—there was a time when I used a considerably "richer" mixture, thinking that "if a little does a little good—a *lot* must do more." My eyes became more red and my fingers more numb, but other than that, the extra didn't seem to do a thing for my work. I could have said to use a "capful," but there are large caps and small ones. An eyedropper holds thirty-five to forty drops, or roughly one-half teaspoonful. Because of the rather pungent odor, I recommend the smallest quantity that I have found to be effective.

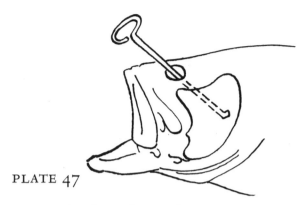

PLATE 47

11. The cheeks again: In an effort to better reach and remove the muscle from the cheeks of his fish, one of my students "discovered" that by thrusting his wire hook through the eye opening into the inner cheek, he could very easily probe and withdraw every scrap through that opening. (See Plate 47.) Sure—whatever does the job! You'll find many innovations of your own to add to your store of information as you go along.

12. Pastes: Formalin has an adverse effect on casein glues and pastes—that is, it causes them to "curdle" in their early setting stages. Elmer's glue is one of these, and although I use it freely in making up bodies, I do *not* use it in pasting up the skin. Any good "school type" paste works well for this; even better are the dextrin-base pastes available from taxidermy supply houses.

13. Carding fins: If you want gently waving curved fins and tail on your fish, fashion your pinning cards from scrap blocks of foam instead of using cardboard. After cutting them to size, split them down the center, giving you two "halves" that fit perfectly and hold the fins as you want them. (See Plate 48.)

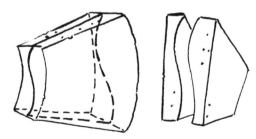

PLATE 48

14. Painting: Too much paint looks far worse than too little! Every beginner has a problem with his color. *Thin* the paint way down with thinner; *wash* in the background colors first and then "touch up" the brighter markings. Keep some clean thinner handy to dip your brush into to keep those colors subdued.

15. Scarcely a week goes by that someone doesn't call to ask how long he or she can keep a fish frozen before having it mounted. If it's kept frozen *solid,* this can be a long time. Dehydration is the most damaging effect on a specimen kept in this state; tails and fins become brittle, stiff, and hard to relax. Wrapping these areas carefully with wet paper towels before freezing is a real help. A fisherman brought in a huge bluegill this summer that he claimed had been frozen for fourteen years! I had no reason to doubt him, for it was completely dehydrated. We relaxed it in plain borax water and then mounted it as a fresh one. It worked out very well, but I must say that I do not recommend such procrastination—I prefer them fresh!

16. Instead of using glue to fasten large blocks of foam together, you can substitute a creamy mix of plaster. Spread it on each piece thinly and press them together. It will "set" in a few minutes and save you much drying time.

ENJOY YOUR WORK—PLEASANT
FISHING!

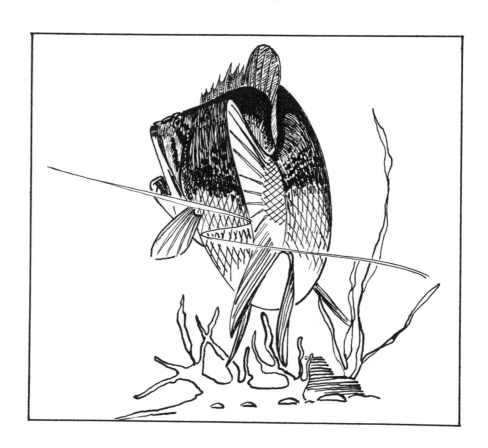